Author's Foreword

This little book is just enough of an overview to give you an idea of the possibilities, realities, and rewards of volunteer prison ministry. It certainly makes no claim to being authoritative or comprehensive. The field of corrections has been thoroughly plowed by scholars, practitioners, and storytellers. Your public library may well have banks of books on the subject, for this underside of life has been well explored.

I have drawn heavily from my own experience as a prison volunteer, but friends in and out of this field have made suggestions, and many inmates have made a major contribution. I have quoted some and included illustrations involving others. The names I have used are fictitious and in some cases the incidents are disguised or combined.

Thanks are due Paul R. Markstrom in charge of Assemblies of God Prison Ministries, who has been active in this field for many years. His influence is felt not only among the chaplains of his own denomination, but also throughout the correctional chaplaincy.

Paul McGarvey, secretary of Men's Ministries of the Assemblies of God, has also been supportive, for he has had a deep interest in a book of this kind to encourage and prepare laymen who are seeking a meaningful personal ministry.

It is doubtful I could write even a pamphlet on the subject without mentioning Burt Pierce, who nudged me into prison ministry, and Niles Behrens, my chaplain pastor.

Elsewhere in the book I pay tribute to Ruth Carter, the mother-in-law I didn't think could make it as a volunteer, and to my wife Nita, my constant prison partner. Inmates assure me they are my chief assets in prison ministry.

—L. C.

LLOYD N. COLBAUGH

THE GOSPEL BEHIND BARS

RadiantBOOKS
Gospel Publishing House/Springfield, Mo. 65802
02-0503

THE GOSPEL BEHIND BARS
© 1979 by the Gospel Publishing House, Springfield, Missouri 65802. All rights reserved. No part of this book may be reproduced, stored in a retrieval system, or transmitted in any form or by any means, electronic, mechanical, photocopy, recording, or otherwise, without prior written permission of the copyright owner, except brief quotations used in connection with reviews in magazines or newspapers.
Library of Congress Catalog Card Number 79-53942
International Standard Book Number 0-88243-503-5
Printed in the United States of America

Contents

1 The Commission 7

2 The Field 14

3 Understanding the Inmate 24

4 Understanding the "System" 39

5 Getting Started 49

6 Working Your Witness 56

7 Accountability 76

8 Follow Up 83

9 The Rewards 92

1
The Commission

Fifteen or so of us were seated in a ragged circle around the smoke-filled room. It could have been a basement room in almost any older church—except for the bars on the windows.

"COMPASSION" was written in capital letters across the top of a blackboard at one end of the room. Under that was "feel with," then "pain," "joy," "fear," and "loneliness."

There were old men and young men; black, white, and Chicano. Most were dressed in khaki. One, in a blue hospital robe, was slouched in a wheelchair. The chaplain was perched casually on a desk by the blackboard. Three of us were Christian volunteers. The rest were inmates in a federal penitentiary.

The conversation had moved from compassion to do-gooders and volunteers. A stocky inmate named Art turned to me. "Why do you come out here? I've been here 3 weeks now and you've been at all these meetings. Why aren't you out bowling, or at home watching TV?"

I squirmed a bit; uncomfortable at being put on the spot, since I hadn't been "coming out" too long.

Then I said the only thing I could think of. "Well, to be honest, the reason I come is because Jesus said, 'I was in prison and you visited me.' " It sounded so pat. So simplistic.

He looked at me sharply. "You really believe that?"

"Yes, I do," I answered.

"Well, where were you 7 years ago when I needed you?" Someone else took up the conversation before I had to reply. I was relieved. (Seven years ago was when Art had become a federal prisoner.)

Without getting into other implications of the words of Jesus in Matthew 25, the passage clearly shows our Lord's ever-present concern for the poor and the oppressed. In fact, He actually identified himself with them. So much so He could say, "When you do it to them, you do it to Me!" Further, this passage teaches us His concern is our concern.

Does this mean we should all become involved in prison ministry? At the least we should all be as open to a call to this kind of service as to any other.

Prisons meet the criteria of any mission field: lost people; a need for laborers; indications of a particular timeliness.

Most people are quick to agree that prisons and jails are full of the lost. The need for laborers seems less apparent. One of the classic appeals made in behalf of missions is, "If we don't go to them, they won't be reached." The prisoner's unique situation surely places him in this category. Many inmates, even before incarceration, live beyond the reach of the average church ministry, separated by class, color, or life-style. This isolation is compounded in prison, as they face society's final rejection.

Shockingly, the rejection many feel most keenly is from the church. Harvey, a drug addict who accepted Christ while "inside," was attempting to develop a satisfactory parole plan. He wrote a minister in his hometown telling him of his conversion and his desire to avoid the pitfalls of his old life should he be released. "Contact me privately if you get out, and I will talk to you. *But don't come to our church!*" was the reply.

Ten pastors in another city were contacted on behalf of an inmate brother. Only one replied, and his letter was less than enthusiastic.

Surely it is unconscionable to close off a mass of sinful men and place them beyond the reach of the gospel. Especially is this true when at the same time we exclude Christian brothers and sisters from our fellowship. For even in prison there are dedicated believers who bear faithful witness, sometimes enduring persecution.

Jimmy reported, "Mr. M------, the officer over our unit, is having me transferred to the psychiatric unit. He says I'm a religious nut because I pray too much."

Jimmy not only prays, he also witnesses faithfully. But the men "inside" cannot do the job alone; nor can the chaplains. For all our American correctional institutions there may be as many as 600 chaplains, including both Catholics and Protestants. Some of these are not spiritually concerned, as we understand it. All are weighed down with paperwork and the supervision of myriad activities unrelated to the gospel. Yet if they were all spiritually diligent and could so devote themselves, even three times the number could not get the job done. If the Lord does not raise up a host of workers, a great harvest may fall, scattered.

It does seem to be God's time for prisons. Ministering in jails and penitentiaries is not new. A faithful few have always been at work behind bars. But there is change in the wind. While the increasing publicity prison ministry is receiving does not necessarily indicate a spiritual timeliness, the fact that God is moving behind the walls does. For years the going was slow, the results meager. Now, not only are new doors opening to Christian ministry in correctional institutions, there is also a new responsiveness to match.

In terms of individual lives, incarceration is often the prime time to sow gospel seed. It represents the bottom. All other hope is gone. Friends have forsaken. Money has run out. The family is breaking up. No wonder "Where Could I Go but to the Lord?" is a popular song among inmates.

Fred stood up in the evening "hymn sing." It was his first time there. It was easy to imagine him as the successful young businessman he said he had been. As he talked it was obvious he had had some acquaintance with the church and Christian principles. "It took this," he said, almost in tears, "to get my priorities back in order. All I wanted was money and the things it could buy my family. Big house, big car—the works. And I did what it took to get it. Now I've lost all that, but I've got my head together. I know now what's really important."

Your response to all this may well be, "Fine. You folks who like this sort of thing and have a knack for it are probably doing a great work. But I don't think I'd fit. I've never been good at passing out tracts or speaking at street meetings. Why, I've never even been to court except for a traffic ticket once! And I could tell then I just didn't fit in with most of those people."

But you *are* reading this book. You do have a gnawing feeling Jesus had a reason for specifically talking about *visiting prisoners*. What if He were to look at you and say, "I was in prison and you didn't visit Me"?

Don't let your past experience, or lack of it, deter you. Don't worry about your personality or your education. You've never had a course in psychology? That may be an asset! You *have* had a course in psychology? Great! God will help you use those insights.

Our team of volunteers has included an ex-marine who sells real estate, a radio announcer, a day laborer out of a job, a hospital business manager, a farm wife, a schoolteacher, a secretary, a great-grandmother, an unemployed musician, a college student from Africa, and one of his college professors.

Perhaps I've put it to you rather strongly. That passage in Matthew percolated in my own mind a long time before I took action on it. I had passed the penitentiary for almost 25 years before I went in. There is a possibility God was working out His own timing, for I was busy many of those years ministering to children.

There are people who can't handle this kind of ministry. One man joined us a number of times. He had an honest concern for people in prison. But he felt a constant constraint—a lack of inner freedom. He decided it was not God's time for him to be in prison ministry. Another, a businessman, found his wife was gripped by fear whenever he left for the institution. Her feelings so complicated his situation that he felt obliged to drop out.

One night at a rap session, Keith sounded off in anger at some visitors who had come to the institution earlier in the week. "You'd think we were in the zoo and they were coming to look at the animals. They think we're freaks of some kind. Not even human!"

Curiosity does inspire some people to participate in a jail ministry for a time or two. But it doesn't sustain them for long. Once the curiosity is satisfied, the "call" can fade rapidly away. There are those, however, who become gripped by the need. With new motivation, they build an enduring ministry.

Inmates are perceptive. They quickly sort out those who are do-gooders, those who are slumming, those who use prisoners to satisfy their own psychological needs. At the conclusion of this chapter is a list of questions you might ask yourself if you are considering jail or prison ministry. All of us need to sort out our motivations. Perhaps this book will help you.

It may open up to you the possibility *your* time to visit people in prison has come.

Questions to Ask Yourself

1. Why would I want to become involved in prison ministry?
2. Is the thought of it frightening? Is it just the idea of the new experience, or am I afraid of physical danger?
3. How could an inmate tell whether I'm a do-gooder* or someone who really cares about him?
4. Could I keep quiet long enough to hear what someone else is saying?

5. How would I answer the man who says, "I don't want to be religious or talk religion. But I need a friend"?

Do-gooder is a derisive term applied to those who do their good works to be seen, particularly when they are patronizing at the same time.

2
The Field

Al had just been transferred from a federal institution to a state penitentiary. "This place is a hellhole. They work people in the field like slaves, a guy with a gun standing over them. Maybe two or three cents an hour. And if we don't have someone send us in clothes, we wear the same stuff day in and day out."

Jim wrote from a west coast institution after spending months in solitary in a midwestern federal penitentiary. "You'd hardly know this is a prison. We can picnic with our visitors—walk with them along the outdoor paths. It blows your mind!"

One night our rap group wandered off the subject—not unusual—and we found ourselves talking about the places men had done time. "The county jails are the worst of all!" "I was gang-raped in a county jail." "You can't believe how crowded it was." It was one of the few times everyone agreed on a subject. All rated county jails at the bottom of their prison experience.

Men may give the same institution opposite ratings, however. George, who had a year or so to do, viewed an institution with a strong community volunteer program as the best place he had been. Herman, who was facing 20 years, was anxious to leave that institution. "I just want to get away and cut off all contact. With the time I have to do, I can't stand rubbing up against the outside world every day. I loved my wife, but when I drew this long sentence, I ran her off. She's only 31 and can make a new life. I couldn't stand it, me being in here and her out there."

These examples spotlight the variety of correctional facilities and the highly subjective way imprisoned people respond to them. Since most who are involved in this kind of volunteer ministry serve only one or two institutions, it would be instructive to overview the major kinds. It may well be you have nearby facilities for confinement that you are hardly aware of.

Names vary, and certain terms are used very loosely by some and more precisely by others. Three different people may call the same institution "prison," "penitentiary," and "correctional facility." Even the official name may not be too helpful—it may have been given for public relations reasons. Most institutions fall into one of these categories: jails, prisons, prison farms or camps, addiction treatment centers, urban correctional centers, work release centers, juvenile homes or detention centers, and halfway houses. The courts also maintain large numbers of people under some degree of control who are not actually imprisoned: through probation and parole, as wards of the court, and by granting release on bond.

This variety of institutions exists for a number of reasons. Multiplicity of jurisdictions is a major reason. Some are federal, others state. Counties and cities maintain separate systems too. The nature of the crime and the situation of the convicted also contribute to the many kinds of facilities. An obvious example is the youthful offender who, solely because of his age, is treated differently from an adult committing the same crime.

Two burglars enter adjacent premises, a retail store and a post office. They steal identical amounts of money. The one will be apprehended, convicted, and confined in a state institution. The post office burglar has committed a federal offense and upon conviction in a federal court will serve his time in a federal facility.

Nick was serving time in a federal prison. He talked hopefully about completing his sentence in June. As June neared, he appeared depressed and asked for prayer. Afterwards, in conversation with a volunteer, he mentioned two detainers. This simply meant two states were waiting their turn either to try him or imprison him. Hoping against hope that time would work in his favor and the actions be dropped, Nick had never mentioned the additional charges. His brave talk about release was only part of the story. In some way, his crime or crimes had straddled federal and state jurisdictions.

Many of the people you may minister to, whatever the facility, are caught like Nick in a tangled web that may involve a number of jurisdictions and institutions before their cases are resolved.

Jails are the entry point for most prisoners. In one crowded facility you may find drunks, a burglary suspect awaiting arraignment, teenage joyriders held on car-tampering charges, a man convicted of rape, an axe murderer who awaits sentencing, and a prominent businessman charged with embezzlement (although he is likely to be out on bond). Psychiatric cases may also be there simply because they present an immediate threat of some kind and there is nowhere else to keep them.

Such a mix is terror for the kept, and frustration—yes, and danger—for the keepers.

The local jail may be city or county. Sometimes it consists of a couple of locked rooms next to the police department. A sophisticated, prisonlike facility may be only one of many jails in a large city. Most counties have some sort of jail. Many are old. Some are makeshift. Most are overcrowded. Administration and staffing are as varied as the facilities. The county sheriff often controls the jail, with one of his deputies serving as jailer. The court may exercise little direct oversight.

The jail in a lightly populated western county is on the top floor of the four-story courthouse, which was built in 1928. The entire building has been well kept and is sound. The jail area is well ventilated, but not air-conditioned. It is reached by narrow stairs and an elevator. The courthouse janitor's living quarters share the same floor. The janitor is deputized as jailer, and his wife is employed as matron and cook. The jail is only occasionally full.

The jail in a larger midwestern city was built as an addition to the courthouse during the Depression. A second-floor enclosed bridgeway joins it to the old building. It has a concrete exercise yard that is seldom used because the manpower is needed to keep order inside. It has some individual cells and several dormitory and tank areas. Each has a toilet and washbowl. A shower room is separate. Jail food is simply another item in the sheriff's budget that must compete with new sirens and radio equipment. The quality varies from week to week and year to year with changes in cooks and sheriffs.

There is one small room where an attorney may consult with a client, or a minister may counsel an inmate. Family visits are carried on by standing in a barred hall. The bars have been boarded up halfway to the ceiling so conversation is through the food slot in the solid iron door. The jail is overflowing. A hum of noise goes on day and night, reaching bedlam level at times.

The newspapers mention the need for new facilities occasionally, when someone is stabbed or hangs himself. Nothing is done.

Jails, except the very large ones, seldom have chapels. They usually have few recreational facilities, no regular chaplains, and no volunteer programs. A minister, however, may almost always visit a specific inmate, particularly if the inmate or his family requests such a visit.

Jails used by the federal prison system as holdover facilities are federally inspected and must meet certain minimum standards. There is often a local visitors' board that inspects a facility once or twice a year to assure the community the jail is not inhumane.

In speaking of state prisons we might properly say "prison system," for at the state level one institution rarely stands alone. It is linked with other facilities. Each serves a specific purpose. There might be, for example, a maximum-security penitentiary. Adjacent to it could be a prison farm where men work under close supervision. Another facility may be called a medium-security prison. There could also be a reformatory for juveniles, an honor camp or farm, and an experimental minimum-security coeducational unit. A small women's prison may complete the system. These institutions will be scattered, often in isolated areas or near small communities.

State systems introduce programs and activities usually limited or unavailable in local jails. Most state systems have full-time professional chaplains. However, not every facility in the system will have a chaplain, or even regular services. In fact, the availability of all programs will likely vary greatly from institution to institution.

Inmates serving long sentences sometimes become part of what is known as the inmate "shadow administration," which exercises unseen but brutal control over other inmates' lives. If the state has additional facilities to transfer inmates who are serving long sentences, the problem is easier to control. But often the state lacks facilities to transfer inmates who become a part of the "shadow administration." Several such power groups in the same prison may contend with each other.

In any institution, local, state, or federal, you must be aware that as a volunteer you contact only one small facet of the real life of the prison. Even in the case of the dedicated Christian inmate you see him within a very limited framework. You have no real concept of what goes on in the areas you never visit, or in the countless hours the people you meet spend away from the religious setting in which you encounter them. There may be grim explanations for sudden absences, abrupt changes of heart, and bitterness between brothers.

Inmates enter the state systems at different levels. Jay was convicted on a felony check charge and sentenced to 3 years. He had been arrested on a drunken spree in another state and brought back to his home county where he was jailed to stand trial. He was a two-time loser. Almost immediately after sentencing he was driven by a sheriff's deputy to the state penitentiary. After a short time in isolation he was assigned a bed and a job.

"I was really scared," he said later. "Somebody puts you to the test right away. There's a sort of pecking order, and they try you to see where you fit in. I moved five times at dinner the first day. If you're eating at a table and a bunch of guys come along and say, 'This is our table!' you move. This place is rough."

Six months later Jay was transferred to a medium-security facility. Things went fairly well and his supervisor liked him. At the end of his first year he was moved to a minimum-security camp, which had once been an army induction center. He was soon given community custody, which meant he could move off the grounds on a pass. Two months later he was granted parole.

Another inmate with a different sort of background might have gone directly to the medium-security facility, even though convicted of the same crime.

Most state systems are caught in a multiple squeeze. Prison administrations are often highly political. Reform groups press for more professional staffing. Courts demand overcrowding be stopped. Some segments of the public push for a "get-tough" policy in the courts, which in turn increases prison population. New institutions are proposed, but no community wants one built near it. The budget crunch compounds every facet of the mess.

This brew of frustration affects every level of prison activity in many states. Administrators and staff feel it. Inmates feel it. State legislatures and governors feel it. You and your volunteer ministry will feel it.

The Federal Bureau of Prisons, a branch of the Justice Department, administers some 40 correctional facilities across the country. Like the state systems, the federal system is made up of a variety of institutions. Some are maximum-security penitentiaries like Marion, a low, modern facility nestled in the southern Illinois countryside; or Leavenworth—the Bigtop—nicknamed for its great central dome, which from a distance makes it look like an imposing turn-of-the-century capitol building. Others are medium- or minimum-security facilities. Some are metropolitan centers—really federal jails. Some serve specialized functions, like the Medical Center for Federal Prisoners in Springfield, Missouri, where we have volunteered for years. It is the hospital for the whole federal prison system, with complete medical and psychiatric facilities. While it is not called a penitentiary, it has provisions for holding all types of prisoners except women.

Alderson, in West Virginia, and Pleasanton in California, house women, while the institutions in Fort Worth, Texas, and Lexington, Kentucky, are coed.

All of the major federal facilities have full-time chaplains and a wide range of religious, educational, and recreational programs.

With such a large number of institutions under one administration, more effective control can be maintained over troublesome situations. Problem inmates and inmates with problems can be transferred to more appropriate facilities.

A Bureau of Prisons bus system, along with the U.S. marshalls, effects the movement of prisoners throughout this national network.

Bureau staff members too are afforded a wide range of experience through transfers within the system.

A variety of satellite activities operate around the fringes of the correctional field. Some are experimental. Some are steps designed to help offenders leave conventional institutions, or avoid incarceration altogether. Work-release programs, halfway houses, court-ordered treatment programs, etc., fall in this class.

Probation and parole activities, while part of the criminal justice system, take us beyond confinement into the area of supervision in the free community.

This is a brief, and by no means comprehensive, view of your prison mission field, with its outpost in your hometown. No matter the obvious differences between institutions, or between classes of inmates—one central theme binds this unique community together: *people confined against their will share an experience the rest of us can never fully understand.*

The volunteer in prison ministry can introduce these people, joined by *shared bondage,* to a vital new set of relationships marked by *shared deliverance.*

Questions to Ask Yourself

1. What is the correctional facility nearest me?
2. Do I know who runs it?
3. Do I have any responsibility in the way it is run?
4. Have I ever talked to anyone who has been confined there?
5. Has my church ever sent a representative there?
6. Should it? Why?
7. How could I go about getting in as a volunteer?
8. Should I be a volunteer?

3

Understanding the Inmate

"I couldn't believe it! They're just people!" We were quizzing a new volunteer about her feelings after her first visit inside the bars. Of course the response is natural. People react the same way when confronted face to face with a television personality, foreigners, or practitioners of strange religions. We are always surprised to find how much alike we all are. There is no way to draw a line between men and women who populate our prisons and the rest of us except one quoted over and over by inmates themselves: "We got caught."

Yet it may be worthwhile demonstrating the variety, for you are likely to express the same surprise as our new volunteer on your first visit.

If you come from a racially sheltered background, you are certain to say to yourself, "Hmmm. Sure a lot of minorities here." You may not sense the variety of *individuals* because you have not had enough association with ethnic groups to see them as other than black, Chicano, or Indian. But if you are past that hurdle, you'll see the whole panorama of totally individual human beings.

Mel is short, stocky, about 35, married, and has three children. He was a Sunday school superintendent, businessman, and youth counselor. He went to a neighboring city and robbed a bank when his businesses started to fail.

Jug is 29. He never knew his mother until he returned from Viet Nam and discovered her name by accident, then went looking for her. Somebody pointed her out to him in a bar where she was hustling customers. His crime—car theft.

Ed, 63, killed his niece's husband in a drunken brawl over the way the younger man treated his wife. He had been a steam fitter until drinking cost him his job.

Elmer sings in the prison choir. He has an unusual voice and knows all the old hymns. He had been a backup singer for a renowned gospel soloist. He was caught dealing drugs on the side from the pharmacy where he handled deliveries.

Hal is a lawyer—or was. His wife is a dedicated Christian now supporting herself and their two children by teaching school. She drives 150 miles each way every Saturday to visit him. Hal started dabbling in real estate promotion when his father left him a farm near a popular resort. He was convicted several years later of violating state fraud laws in a stock scheme set up to push a new lakeside development.

Arlen, 30, has been in institutions of one kind or another since he was 14. His sister overdosed on drugs. His father and two brothers are in state and federal penitentiaries. The mother is a hopeless alcoholic.

The descriptions could go on and on—colorful, sordid, tragic. If you aren't careful, you'll find yourself caught up in the fascination of the stories instead of listening for the needs.

Not all of the personal biographies you hear are true. Prison creates a need for impressive credentials. Del told about an experience he had while serving time. A hometown acquaintance had been brought in on some sort of bank conviction. Del heard him describing a daring robbery, with drawn guns and a big haul. This went on for some time, with the newcomer telling and retelling the story, reinforcing his image as a tough, daring desperado. Later it was in Del's self-interest to cut the new man down to size. He produced a clipping from their home paper detailing the crime: It had actually been a nighttime burglary that netted small change from a cash drawer. The attempt had been bungled, resulting in the immediate arrest of—who else—the daring "robber"!

Another aging inmate, Frank L., was known by all to be the heir of a renowned automobile pioneer. His family name had been made famous by the turn-of-the-century luxury sports cars which bore it. At least it appeared to be Frank's name, for everyone, including guards, called him Mr. L. His actual records revealed no evidence to support his claims, and after his death inside prison no one stepped forward to claim either his body or his "fortune."

During a long association, Harry had told us many stories of his past, including his childhood. Some of these stories were supposed to explain why he was what he was. But they left us with an uneasy feeling they didn't all fit. After he made a Christian profession, we asked Harry which stories were the truth. "Well, it may take a long time to get it all straight," he said. "I don't remember exactly what I told you, and some things I've told so many times I'm not even sure myself anymore."

How do you sort out all the people and all the stories in the relatively brief contacts you have as a volunteer? You can't. You are not there as judge, psychiatrist, or therapist. Your concern goes beyond the surface, real or phony, to the hurting man or woman, offering the balm Jesus brings. Follow this course and you will not be embarrassed by having been overly impressed by an inmate's biography that proves to be false.

In the last chapter we mentioned how differently people respond to the prison experience. When Jack was brought in (again) you would have thought it was old home week. He immediately dropped into all the old routines and relationships. He was "con-wise" (a bit of jargon meaning he knew the system, the ways of fellow inmates and guards). Jack may well be institutionalized—unable to function except within the rigid framework of prison. Some observers state that most men confined over 3 or 4 years have an impaired capacity to function apart from an institutional setting.

Andy was something else entirely. A man about 50, I first encountered him one evening when we approached the chapel area. Chairs lined the wide hall separating the chapel from the chaplains' office. Men waiting to see the chaplains, or simply seeking escape from the prison atmosphere, use the hall almost as a lounge area. Andy was sitting in one of the chairs at the end, separated from the others by racks of books and tracts. My attention was drawn by his look of dejection. I was sure I had never seen him before.

I approached quietly and introduced myself. He

stood, his head still down. As he shook my hand he gave me his name. Suddenly his face contorted as he tried to hold in the sobs. He had been a contractor who ran afoul when he started dealing with the government. His family was in distress. He was at the point of suicide. He saw no hope, no meaning. It was his first night in a penitentiary, far from home. Up until sentencing he had been out on bond. I had walked up on him at the low point of his life. It proved to be the turning point, for from that time on he began to rearrange his values. Six months later he left new—in his relationship to Christ, in his plans for the future, and in his understanding of himself.

In between Jack and Andy are all shades of response to being in prison. Some withdraw—they read no books, listen to no news. Prison is a dead space, a parenthesis in their lives. You will likely not see them, for they avoid all contacts, particularly with outsiders.

Many, perhaps most, live with fear. Fear is a powerful molding force. It shapes many of the relationships that develop inside the walls. First, it is responsible for the shells—the false fronts—inmates hide behind. It is important to establish oneself in the hierarchy of fear early in the game, so most inmates come on tough. The weaker ones become the tools of the stronger in relationships dictated by fear. These relationships may be sexual, or they may involve a whole range of favors having nothing to do with sex. An extra pack of cigarettes, pressed pants from the laundry, or protection may be exchanged for loyalty in various enterprises and conflicts.

Naturally there are inmates who can't cope with such a system and they seek protection, not from stronger inmates, but from the administration. A civil right even a prisoner can claim is the right to life. No prison administrator wants to come up with a murdered man on his hands. It is particularly embarrassing if it can be demonstrated the man sought protection and none was given. So inmates are often placed in protective units at their own request.

The man who reacts to prison life by becoming a tattler or informer takes the most precarious route of all. He violates a code everyone understands—you don't see anything, you don't hear anything. You keep your nose out of other people's business. Once a man has the reputation of being a snitch, he has a hard row to hoe. The reputation follows him through the inmate grapevine from institution to institution. He may lose his life or spend his time in protective custody.

Incidentally, the inmate grapevine is a very real factor in prison life. Our mobile society, in tandem with the multiple conviction records of many inmates, means even state institutions are "plugged in" to this underground communications line.

If you were to examine some inmates' jackets (files) you might find them identified as "manipulators." While some respond to prison life by avoidance and others by playing it tough, the manipulators manage by their wits. They likely were "confidence men" on the outside. They simply adapt those skills to the inside, exercising them on inmates, staff, and visitors alike. They may be charming and affable. While many are relatively nonviolent, some don't seem to mind a reputation among their fellows of possessing certain deadly skills.

Mike was a giant of a man who had been involved in street gangs on the outside. He was making a less than wholehearted attempt to change his life-style. He attended most chapel services and religious activities, but occasionally he would simply stand outside the door looking morose and overwhelmed by discouragement. He was being hassled back in his ward about his Christian involvement.

"Look, man," he said one night, "don't look for me no more. You're a good dude. But I'm not coming back here. This guy has just pushed me too far and I don't have to take it. I can't go back to my old neighborhood and live like you say anyhow. I'm gonna get this guy. This place can't do anymore to me anyhow. What do I got to lose?"

Mike was flirting with a kind of sellout, a living suicide. He had nothing to go back to outside. (His family was dead.) He felt he had experienced the worst the inside had to inflict. So why restrain himself? Even murder was meaningless.

How do you respond? I certainly wasn't going to make any instant psychiatric diagnosis. That was not my role. I had prayed for this man. I had prayed *with* him. Now I prayed silently as he spoke. Mostly I just listened and gripped his hand as he turned to leave. The next week he was back—smiling! Actually, I have no way of knowing whether he really had planned to abandon his shaky faith and go kill a man, or he had simply wanted desperately for someone to care so he used this approach to coax a little extra time and attention from a volunteer.

The incident illustrates how inextricably the inmate's response to the prison experience may be bound to his response to you. And just as there is an endless spectrum of ways to adapt to prison life, there will be a variety of reactions to you.

Expect to be tested at the outset—not once, but

many times. Perhaps as many times as there are inmates; for no one will fully accept another's report of where you are coming from at face value.

"What's your angle?" is always the unspoken question. Often it's the *spoken* question as well.

"Are you a preacher?" may be translated in a number of ways. It is a way of asking, "Do you get paid for this?" If you get paid for it, that explains why you are there. You don't have a real interest in inmates. You're a mercenary. You're like all church people—phony, in it for the money. Yet the same question may be a way of asking, "Do you have any authority? Do you really know what you're talking about? I want to talk to someone who really knows."

"Do you work here?" may be an innocent question to pass the time of day. It may also serve to categorize you as "one of them." A spy for the institution. Also a paid phony.

There are many other ways to probe your motivation. Inmates want to sort out real people from do-gooders. If they think they will simply become more scalps on your church belt, they are turned off. "I'm only interested in souls," may be a way of saying, "I'm not really interested in *you*."

Do you show an inordinate interest in an inmate whose name and crime have been in the news? Another cloud on your motivation. You are just a sensation seeker.

There is good reason for inmates to check people out. Prisons are full of men and women who have been hurt by life, perhaps again and again. Your coming presents one more opportunity for being hurt.

Our Thursday night group included a lot of old-timers, both inmates and volunteers, who knew each other well. We fell to discussing how they, the inmates, reacted to us, the volunteers. (Maybe we were just looking for some kind words. Even volunteers crave positive strokes now and then!) Sam enlightened us. "You folks do come on a little strong sometimes. Now *we* know where you're coming from. It's great. But some poor new guy who has never met anybody like you, especially in this place—wow! He's overwhelmed. You come on with big smiles and handshaking and backpatting. 'What have I gotten into?' he's asking himself. 'What's their angle? And all this love bit. The only times I've ever opened myself to love, I've been clobbered.' "

We learned it's possible to be more threatening by being warm and open than if we were more reserved. But when we suggested changing our style, it was a different story. "Stay like you are. Them guys'll find out you're for real," Sam assured us.

There is a problem, however. How is the man whose own mother and father have betrayed him, whose only romantic experiences have been on a cash basis, whose partners in crime have sold him out—how is that man going to handle a perfect stranger coming up and saying, "I love you. I am concerned that you're hurting"? Yet it is essential to get beyond the protective walls, so Christ's love— the love that heals—can flow in.

The terminology of love and caring relationships that seems so natural to believers can be misconstrued in the prison setting. The warm embrace of Christian brothers can elicit, "Man, look at them weirdos hug!"

The testing goes beyond checking out your motivations. You represent a valuable potential to be cultivated and used. You are a possible access to the world outside.

The inmate knows you are forbidden to carry contraband in or out. His testing is to see whether you will or not. Often it starts on an inconsequential level: get an address; make a phone call. Many times it would never go beyond that. Yet even so you compromise your credibility if you acquiesce. Far more serious, you may set yourself up for continued manipulation, even blackmail.

In spite of all the negative ways of relating you do carry with you a dynamic rare in many inmates' lives that makes you positively attractive. You are a good, clean, upright success.

As Bob said, "I like to be seen with you. To have you stop and talk with me gives me status. Not just with other inmates. With myself. I know somebody who is making it in life. And they care about me enough to spend time with me."

Many of your most promising contacts may be made first at this level, casually talking and sharing, quite apart from the preaching and singing.

We have discussed differing ways inmates respond to the prison experience and to you, the volunteer. Religion sparks a similar variety of reactions.

You just know some inmates were professional exploiters of religion on the outside. Typical is Willie. "What denomination are you? You sound holiness." You identify your church. "Oh, do you know Brother Sims, pastor over on Eighth and Sentinel? And what was the man's name who pastored the other little church in Brookdale. . . ?"

You look at Willie and begin to doubt he ever was in a church. Then it occurs to you he just may have been one of those who go the rounds of church offices getting "help for my destitute family," or "money for gas to get back to my children in Little Rock." Then there are the perennial seekers who respond to every altar call—a big boost for ministers that deal in the statistics of conversions. Sometimes it is a lack of understanding of what conversion is all about. In many cases the man has lived like a sinner since his last profession and wants the "good feeling" again. Others are so anxious to please you they come simply because they think it's what you want. Patience and careful follow-up may help such people.

Hecklers come in many guises. They can come to a Bible class as earnest students and then disrupt by asking all the unanswerable questions. In a sharing session they can pour out lurid tales of scandal and greed encountered in churches outside. Testimony time may turn into a diatribe against some of the professing Christians in the institution who "come down here and pretend to be Christians, then go back and live like the devil."

Garland was a lesson in never giving up. For years he whipsawed our religious programs. He would participate glibly, quoting Scripture and singing hymns. Then he would lambast the chaplain and all the "hypocrites—I can't stand them." When we suggested he was the biggest of all, Garland replied, "I sell it. I don't buy it."

In spite of his games we welcomed him in Christian love. But it seemed hopeless. Then at last the Holy Spirit broke through his sham and Garland made a genuine commitment.

There is always someone who asks, "What about Billy Graham and his pal Nixon?" Or, "How come all these churches are so rich and there are little kids starving?"

You'll be surprised at the *religious* people in prison. Some have taken dozens of Bible correspondence courses. Others are "ministers" with credentials by mail. The confusion that results often creates problems. A brother participating eagerly in a Bible class may sound quite orthodox. Then as he continues his doctrine takes a strange shift, weaving in ideas from a far-out cult. "Oh, I go to all the religious groups. Muslims, Christian Science, TM. I figure there's good in 'em all. I sort of have my own beliefs. Did you ever read Edgar Cayce? I'm really into reincarnation." About then you feel more comfortable with the man who makes no profession at all.

After encountering the endless variety of people in prison you will find yourself seeking some common threads, some categories to help you come to grips with this separated world. If you have done much reading you know there are sociologists, psychologists, and psychiatrists who have devoted their professional lives to analyzing criminals and crime. They come to differing conclusions.

It is no doubt presumptuous then for us to venture opinions. One word creeps up again and again, however, as we think about the hundreds of inmates we have observed through the years: *immaturity*. It doesn't explain anything; it is simply descriptive.

What are the evidences of immaturity? There is frequently a low threshold of response: anger flares quickly and is expressed directly with little regard for the consequences. There is a demand for instant gratification, whether the need is money, sex, acclaim, or whatever. Slow, patient striving toward goals seems difficult, if not impossible. There is a reluctance to accept responsibility for one's actions. Recent social theory has somewhat abetted this latter attitude. Many inmates are happy to accept the judgment that society is at fault for them being what they are. Of course, if there is no responsibility, there is no guilt, and if there is no guilt, there is no need for Christ.

The other side of the coin is that if there is no responsibility, all are victims of circumstance and there is no hope. The doctrine that we are all puppets of chance offers little encouragement to the man or woman on the bottom of the heap.

Life in prison does nothing to encourage maturity, with the single exception that it offers time for reflection. The inmate is told when to go to bed and when to get up. He has no control over what he wears, what he eats, or what he spends. In many cases he is not only treated as a child—he is also thought of as a child. Scarcely a climate for personal growth.

While there may be doubt about what constitutes the "criminal type," there is little doubt about the effects of the prison experience that most inmates share.

A high percentage of family relationships fail to survive incarceration. The "Dear John" letter is common. Divorce laws make it easy. Conviction is automatically grounds for divorce. In a number of states a consummated marriage can be annulled for a few dollars if a partner to the marriage is convicted of a felony. Some families are so humiliated they completely cut off communication with the imprisoned member. Children grow up never knowing their father.

Chris' wife was killed prior to his incarceration. Their son was only a toddler when Chris left him with the wife's parents to go to prison. Years later the grandparents and son surprised Chris with a visit—a seemingly generous gesture. He was overjoyed; except for one thing. "They introduced me to my own son as 'Uncle Chris.' All these years and he hasn't even known I was his daddy."

Even when a family struggles to stay together, prison leaves a bitter legacy. The wife and mother has full responsibility as head of the home. She suffers immeasurably for a crime she didn't commit. Then the father is released and comes home to assume his role. He may very well find he isn't needed. His wife may be reluctant to accept her husband as the head of the household. This creates a traumatic situation for the family unit. It's a strong spouse who can avoid throwing up the past in some moment of stress or conflict.

As common as the breakup of the family is the loss of self-esteem. No matter the inmate's bold manner and his tough, boastful words. Society has rendered its verdict: "You are worthless. We don't want you around where we have to associate with you." Such inner feelings can easily be translated, "Since I'm so worthless *people* don't want me, it's certain I'm on *God's* trash heap too."

Bernie, a handsome man of about 60, was led to a sharing group by another inmate. He kept his head lowered as he shuffled in. Never once did he look up, even when we were introduced. Naturally he said nothing in the group meeting. But in personal conversation he haltingly spilled out his contempt for himself and his unworthiness before God. Even later after he had accepted the Lord, he prefaced every comment and prayer with a litany of unworthiness.

It is not hard to recognize loss of self-esteem in a man like Bernie. Those who cover it with toughness and cynicism are harder to identify as fellow-sufferers of this prison malady. Often it is at the brink of Christian commitment their sense of failure surfaces. "How," they ask, "can I succeed in this new life when I have failed in everything else I've ever done?" If the question is sincere, it may be the opening you need to gently lead him to a perception of his worth before God.

Your task as a volunteer in prison will not be to beat men over the head with their sinfulness. You will find yourself praying instead for the words to express the universality of God's love, and the value He places on all the lost.

Questions to Ask Yourself

1. Draw a picture of a typical criminal.
2. Are you good at detecting lies? How do you do it?
3. What would you do if you discovered an inmate you had been dealing with for several weeks had been consistently lying to you?
4. Would you do a small against-the-rules favor for an inmate if he promised to read the Bible in return?
5. Do you believe some people have weak characters?
6. Shouldn't we all have a strong sense of unworthiness?

4
Understanding the "System"

The "system" has become the whipping boy of the last couple of decades. The term obviously has many meanings. There is one usage in which it has come to include all aspects of handling crime and criminals. More precisely, we talk about the criminal justice system. Although system is hardly the word if by it you mean order and coherence. Our whole approach to handling crime and criminals is in a state of confusion and flux.

There are serious conflicts in purpose; grave doubts in the public mind. What are we trying to accomplish through our courts? punishment? revenge or retribution? deterrence? rehabilitation? or some combination? You may hear much discussion about goals, methods, and facilities. It will be useful to you to keep abreast of the direction the "system" is going.

Keep in mind that at the level you encounter the system—the jail or prison—the bottom line is one word: *custody*. The administration of a jail or prison has one overriding commitment: *Do not lose* the men or women placed in your care. Everything else takes a backseat to the concerns of custody or security. You think of how valuable it would be to take a new convert with you to church outside. It would greatly encourage him. The church people could become acquainted with him and hold him up in prayer. On the other hand, the prison administration thinks of all the possibilities of escape.

Phil and Dave had been spending a lot of time around the chapel. They had also developed a good relationship with a social worker in the institution. No services of their faith were being held inside the institution. Phil and Dave expressed a deep desire to worship with a local congregation of their persuasion. The social worker was not religious at all, but a caring sort of man, so he arranged to escort both men to a service. At a convenient break Phil and Dave went to the restroom. The social worker didn't see Phil and Dave again. At a later hearing he was docked 2 week's pay for his error in judgment.

If you made a request of that institution to take an inmate friend to church, you would have the hurdle of past bad experience to clear. The administration would feel it had good reason to say "no."

One adverse experience may affect many institutions. After an escape from a prison visiting room in the West involving a hostage, visiting room procedures were tightened all across the country.

You may respond to the talk of custody by protesting that you don't want to take anyone out. You simply want to come in. What you must recognize is *your* presence in the institution is also a custodial concern, and a legitimate one. The staff must provide for your safety. You are an added distraction to occupy the attention of a limited staff.

While outside visitors are an asset, and the programs you sponsor undoubtedly release tensions and contribute to the well-being and contentment of the inmate population, these pluses must be balanced against the extra concern your visit causes. If an institution is troubled with a contraband problem—illegal materials coming inside—every increase in traffic from outside means one more opportunity for violation.

Many local jails are so crowded they have no real facilities for handling religious volunteers. What may appear to be callous disregard for inmates' spiritual needs may simply reflect a desperate situation in housing and manpower.

As we will discuss in the chapter on getting started, most prison and jail administrations consist of a number of "layers" of authority and responsibility. At the county jail level the sheriff is usually in charge. In a small county the next in line may be the deputy who is jailer. In a large county there may be a complicated organizational structure, including a chaplain responsible for coordinating religious activities.

State and federal systems are also highly organized. Each federal institution has a warden, or superintendent who exercises considerable discretion within general policy guidelines. Under him will be an associate. Captains have direct oversight of custody. Next in line are the lieutenants, and then the correctional officers (as the guards are called).

Each institution has a cadre of social workers—case managers—who handle the relationships of inmates to the institution, to parole boards, etc. They monitor progress, sit in on staff consultations regarding specific inmates, and take care of much of the paperwork each inmate generates. Food services, records, industry, education, and maintenance all have their boxes on the organizational chart, as well as complements of managers and workers. One accusation of critics is that prisons are big businesses that profit an overgrown, well-paid bureaucracy as well as the adjacent communities.

All the religious activities are under the supervision of the chaplain. Most federal chaplains are full-time employees of the Bureau of Prisons, meeting high educational standards. An advisory committee of denominational representatives interviews candidates and makes recommendations. A candidate must of course have the approval of his own denomination. A typical institution will have a Catholic chaplain and a Protestant chaplain. But under their supervision will be services for Mormons, Jehovah's Witnesses, Christian Scientists, World Community of Islam in the West, Moorish Science Temple, and Jews. The chaplain's office may also distribute greeting cards, help arrange phone calls, sponsor seminars and retreats, and coordinate toy distributions at Christmas.

Wherever there is a chaplain, he will be your key contact. Some effort to understand his situation will facilitate your ministry. First, if he is a full-time government employee, he is confronted with a multiple role. He must represent his employer. He must be true to his own religious convictions. He must have the interest of the inmates at heart. Because the inmate considers the government the adversary, he must perceive the chaplain as being apart from that adversary relationship. Otherwise the chaplain will lose credibility or be considered a "cop." The chaplain is the only one in the institution who is in this unique position. He must truly be "all things to all people."

His role as a religious activities coordinator is difficult. The chaplain arranges for ministries of many different faith groups, some of which may be in conflict with the aims of his own outreach. Finally, he is chaplain to the members of the institution's staff; a role that may take him outside to hospitals, funerals, and counseling sessions.

Chaplains are as varied as the pastors in your hometown. Some are strongly evangelistic. Some are charismatic. Some are liberals. Some are liturgical. And some seem little more than social workers.

You may be able to establish a warm working relationship with the chaplain. On the other hand, he may be so averse to your church background that he classes you with cults whose activities he must grudgingly tolerate. Frank and open discussion will prevent misunderstandings and help maintain a satisfactory working relationship, even if you have no real sense of fellowship.

Whoever made the decision to admit your ministry into the jail or prison—the chaplain, jailer, or other official—you still will come in direct and regular contact with the custodial staff. Although the warden himself has welcomed you, don't be dismayed if others show less enthusiasm or even resistance. Some people may exasperate you with their nitpicking attendance to rules; their apparent determination to thwart your ministry by worrying it to death exercising their low-level authority.

Experiments with a group of college students gave some insight into this kind of behavior. Half of the group was picked at random to be jailers, the other half, prisoners. Even though everyone was aware of what was going on, the jailers became demanding and abusive. When the roles were reversed, the ex-prisoners were just as insufferable as their former jailers had been.

When you intrude upon a system where one group survives (literally) by constantly asserting its authority, don't be surprised if a little officiousness splashes over on you. If a situation becomes unbearable, follow the rules all institutions abide by: observe the chain of command. In other words, report your problems quietly to the individual you are directly responsible to.

When a case comes to trial, it is entered on the records as "The State versus John Doe." That adversary relationship continues long after the final gavel ends the court sessions. However varied their backgrounds and personalities, inmates are remarkably unified on one thing. It's still "us against them." They live in a world controlled by the enemy. You enter the arena as a possible ally. There will be efforts to recruit you in the battle.

A scrawny, toothless, rumpled little man fell in beside me as we walked down the ramp leading from the chapel area. "I don't have nobody. You're a Christian. You people believe in helpin', don'tcha? You know, I shouldn't be in here. I didn't do *nothin.*' Could you talk to the newspaper or the civil liberties people for me? They say I threatened the president. I couldn't a done that. I was passed out dead drunk. Don't remember a thing."

Was he anxious for justice, or simply access to a bottle?

Sometimes your righteous anger will be stirred. The young black man sitting in the small group meeting had drawn 5 years for his crime. Sitting near him was another man soon to finish his 6 months for a similar crime involving a much greater amount of money. The two men had been tried and sentenced in different courts.

How do you respond to claims of innocence or injustice? Be honest. Don't give false hope. Don't make promises you can't keep. Don't make a judgment—you don't have all the facts. You may be deeply moved, perhaps totally convinced. But take care. You could respond: "What you are telling me sounds like it is hurting you very deeply. I am not taking it lightly. I will give it thought and prayer. In the meantime, I have a serious proposition to present back to you for your thought and prayer. If we let Him, God will use even the injustices of life to help us grow. While You're working for justice, don't let bitterness destroy you. Have you ever really given any thought to what *God* might want for you?"

Discuss any such matter with the chaplain or your group leader. Becoming involved on your own opens you to the possibility of spending many hours of time and effort that can end in heartache and disillusionment.

Occasionally, especially in a jail setting, you will get a request from someone to post bond for him. "It's only $500 and you'll get it all back because I'm not going anyplace—my family just needs me desperately right now. My wife is about to have a baby. . . ." This may be an excellent opportunity for your church to minister to the wife. But becoming a bondsman is a lot like investing in the stock market. Don't do it if you can't afford to lose it.

"Will you write the judge. . . ? the parole board. . . ?" These are frequent requests. But ask yourself how much you can honestly say: "I met Joe last week. We talked for 10 minutes and he bowed his head and prayed the sinner's prayer with me. I saw him again today and he seemed to be doing great. Said he was really going to live a new life outside. Please consider this when you are weighing your sentence. Sincerely, a religious worker you never heard of." You can see that unless there was a lot more to it than that, your recommendation would carry little weight!

However much you want to please and encourage someone, don't be afraid to be honest. A real conversion will survive honesty. Simply say, "Joe, we are only starting to know each other. I must be honest. I do trust God though. I'm going to join with you in prayer, committing the entire matter to Him. Then, whatever happens, we'll know it's part of His long-range plan."

The most difficult matter of all to deal with is the report of brutality. The news may come quietly. You ask, "Where's Tommy who was with us last week? Did he go home?"

"He's in insolation. The guards worked him over Monday . . . broke his nose."

You feel disbelief, embarrassment, then shame. The disbelief may be because you have reason to question the credibility of the one speaking, or simply because you don't *want* to believe. The embarrassment comes because it was your question that prompted the unpleasant disclosure. The shame is generated by the thought that in your institution such means would be used to deal with problems. And shame also because of your own sense of powerlessness.

But what do you *say*? "I'm sorry. May the Lord

forgive us all. Let's pray for Tommy and for the guards involved." Of course, you must never forget you have heard only one side of the story.

You will notice the suggested approach to each of the dilemmas of involvement I've mentioned is prayer. The inmate may say, "That's a cop-out. Anytime you don't want to *do* something, you say 'Let's pray!'" Any religious exercise can be a "cop-out." The ancient Israelites preferred to sacrifice calves than to obey. But if you view prayer as a dynamic force in the Christian arsenal and you hold yourself open, ready for God to act in you and through you, you don't have to make apologies for taking the path of prayer.

This chapter opened by noting the criminal justice system is in flux; many opposing views are seeking to shape it. You will be challenged both by inmates and by groups in the community to change the character of your involvement. Over a period of years our small-group sessions had become a sounding board for several very vocal inmates. Ken was a big burly guy who, while admitting he had absolutely no twinges of conscience about any act he had ever committed, still had a keenly honed sense of the way Christians should behave. "How," he said, "can you come in here preaching to us about love and righteousness and God's goodness, then go out and not do anything about changing these hellholes we inmates have to exist in?" He would document his characterization with a long recital of abuses.

Ken had a point. It was one I had given a lot of thought to, for through the years I have regularly read publications from prison activist groups. "I *am* an activist, Ken," I replied. "You may not be satisfied with my style, but I am not sitting at home. I am here.

A long time ago I had to choose a direction. I could march up and down outside these walls with a sign, or I could forego that role and come inside. I am in here at the 'system's' sufferance and I don't think they would have let me have it both ways. I feel God wants me here."

I don't accept people putting me down because my way of meeting a need in the world is different from theirs. By the same token, I won't put them down by saying, "Oh, our way is better than yours. *We're* interested in *souls!*"

You will have to choose your way of responding to the great social problems of crime and punishment as God leads *you*.

Questions to Ask Yourself

1. What are prisons for?
2. How would you feel if you were imprisoned unjustly and you couldn't get outside volunteers to take you seriously?
3. What are the advantages of having chaplains in institutions?
4. Do you look down on prison guards? Is being a guard as respectable as being a policeman or a judge?
5. When you read about a daring and clever prison escape attempt, do you find yourself rooting for the prisoners?
6. What if there were no prisons?

5

Getting Started

You've just dropped the evening paper in your lap and you are about to settle down to watch TV for the evening. An item in the daily record section draws your eyes back down to the paper: "Jeffrey Jenkins, age 19, was sentenced to 3 years in the state penitentiary for breaking and entering with intent to commit a felony."

In the past you've never bothered to look at such trivia. But you've been skimming through this book occasionally, and a sense of restlessness has been coming over you as you sit in your pew each week.

You look at the item again. Nineteen years old. Three years out of the very prime of his life to be spent locked up with men more experienced in crime than he. You don't even know the kid. You pick up your Bible from the table beside you and turn to Matthew 25. Those words you've read so often rise up from the page: "I was in prison, and you visited me."

For the first time in your life you feel called. You really feel called. But how do you answer? How can you be sure? Don't be embarrassed. Remember how

Samuel first answered? "What do you want, Eli?" When the call persisted, Samuel got some advice from the priest: "Say, 'Speak, Lord.'"

Actually this chapter is not really about how you get a call to prison ministry, or how you can be sure. God speaks in so many ways it would be presumptuous to suggest how He's going to get your ear. The question we will deal with is the next step after the call: "How do I get started?"

If there is already a prison ministry in your church, the answer is easy. Go to the leader and volunteer. If there is not, the next step is still easy. Go talk with your pastor and share your concern with him. You are about to become involved in a mission field, so you will need the interest and support of a home base.

Consultation with your pastor is important for several reasons. First, it is simply common courtesy. As a member of the church he pastors you will in effect be a church representative. He needs to know who is doing what in the name of the church. Second, he may already have plans underway for a jail or prison ministry. Your individual effort might compromise them. On the other hand, your cooperation could be just the impetus needed to start the project moving. Finally, you may very well need your pastor to speak for you. Whether you agree with it or not, a fact of life around institutions is that a credentialed minister has an entree even the most dedicated layman does not have.

If your pastor seems less than eager, don't be discouraged. Ask for an appointment to discuss it with him more fully. In your meeting with him, explore some of these questions:

Do you feel I am ready for this kind of ministry? If not, how can I prepare myself?

Do you have other plans for prison ministry that would make my moving now inappropriate or in conflict?

Are you hesitant because you fear you will have to spend extra time? Perhaps if you help me get started I can arrange to share some other part of your load.

Are you concerned that this involvement will divide my interest, and consequently lessen my value to the church? Doing what I feel called to do will deepen my commitment and make me *more* worthwhile. Just consider that you're not losing a member, you're gaining a missionary.

He may be legitimately concerned about your church attendance, for he recognizes the necessity of "taking in" before "giving out."

Once the pastor has agreed to work with you, you might share this chapter and the following one with him.

The next question in starting a new prison ministry is, "Whom do we see?" If the institution has a chaplain, you have your answer—all religious activities are channeled through him. No matter where you started, you'd eventually be saying, "Chaplain, we're interested in volunteer ministry in this institution."

If there is no chaplain, the question may well be answered with a question, "Whom do you know?" If you or the pastor are well acquainted with a sympathetic public official, start with him. Don't say, "Get us into the jail." Rather say, "We are interested in starting a prison ministry. What would be the proper channel? Would it be appropriate for us to use your name in making the approach?"

If you don't know anyone, a good rule of thumb is

to start at the top and work down. Get *your* top man—the pastor—to do the talking.

Keep alert to political nuances. If you've been reading in the papers that the county judge and the sheriff are wrangling over the budget and aren't speaking, don't go to the sheriff and say, "Judge Smith sent us."

In fact, it is wise to brief yourself ahead of time on as many facts about the institution as possible. A newspaper reporter on the police beat can give you some idea of what's going on. Should the institution be going through troublesome times with changes of staff or internal strife, it might be wise to put it on your prayer list and hold off awhile. If such problems are chronic, you might as well push ahead; otherwise you'll never get started.

Once you have some idea of the situation you're approaching, develop some plans. Decide on how many are going, or would like to go. Take an inventory of their talents. Have a preliminary meeting for prayer and organization.

If your preliminary research revealed some special need in the institution, create a plan to fill that need. Should you be dealing with a chaplain, your initial contact might feel him out on his perception of needs in his program: "Chaplain Barth, I'm Mike Leonard. I'm calling for Pastor Brown of Christian Life Center. We have had a developing desire to become involved in prison ministry. Do you have areas of particular need where we might serve? And could we schedule a time when we can meet with you?"

If he seems to have a full program and no needs, don't drop the matter. Say, "That's great, chaplain. You know, we'd still like to get better acquainted with you and your ministry. Could you have lunch with me one day next week?" You might even get the pastor to invite him to speak at your church.

Then get your group together and work out some possibilities to present—ways in which you might make a real contribution to the chaplain's program. Here's a partial list:

Individual witnessing and counseling. You would be prepared to provide a specific number of two-man teams, at times to be arranged or to be on call. The teams would be prepared to witness, counsel on spiritual matters, or encourage and build up believers.

Special music. You would provide special music for a specific date, or regularly. You would provide a regular pianist for services already being held. You would provide a leader for an inmate choir and several "seed" singers to help get it started.

Visitors. You would arrange for visitors to spend time with men who get no visits.

Bible study. You would provide a small team to conduct a regular Bible study. Possible subjects for a study series: The Way of Salvation; Getting Acquainted With the Bible; I'm a New Christian—Now What? or Christianity in Action.

Sharing time for charismatics. You would provide community leadership. (Some institutions have a demand for services of this type. A non-Pentecostal chaplain may be happy to have someone else come in and lead.)

Extension courses. You would bring in extension Bible-study courses, then collect the workbooks, grade, and return them. (The Institutional Chaplaincies of the Assemblies of God is a valuable resource in this area, as well as in many other aspects of prison ministry. They have free Bible courses available.)

Literature distribution or supply. You would provide a religious library service. You would keep reading racks stocked with Christian periodicals and tracts. You would come in regularly and distribute literature to individuals.

Films. Your group would come in once every month to show a gospel film and conduct a response period afterwards.

Rap group. You would supply moderators and some of the participants for weekly rap groups with a religious slant.

Your group may have other special talents such as puppetry or Christian drama. Choose areas you could best serve and draw up your proposal. Whether you are talking with a chaplain, a sheriff, or a social director, you will have something specific to discuss. Don't be overly ambitious. It is better to agree on one avenue of ministry and do a good job than to spread yourself too thin and then retreat.

In your discussion, establish a time. Have complete understanding of all the ground rules. How many are coming? How should they dress? What items may be taken inside? (For example: Purses, Bibles, musical instruments, coats.) If in doubt, ask.

When you recruit your team, get people who will make long-term commitments. A ministry that can count its tenure in years gains credibility and respect.

A couple of questions yet remain. What if you can't get in at all? If you can't find a way in and you still feel deeply burdened, try an end run. If you have the skills, arrange to go in as a secular volunteer— vocational teacher, educational aide, or counselor—or seek employment in the institution. A caring Christian jailer is something else! Another avenue of service that will give you direct access to people in prison is a ministry to the families of the incarcerated. It is a demanding field, but the needs are often greater than those inside the bars.

Finally, what if you are all alone? You don't have a team. The pastor can't help. Yet the call still burns. Many of the approaches and suggestions we have made still hold good. You may simply face more obstacles than if you represented, or were part of, an organized group.

As one of our inmate friends said after a bureaucratic entanglement had delayed our arrival at the prison chapel, "There you guys are trying to get in, and here we are trying to get out!"

Questions to Ask Yourself

1. What's the difference between a call and my Christian conscience?
2. Do I have a history of starting projects, then dropping them? Have I ever stuck with any ministry (such as Sunday school teaching) more than a year?
3. Have I discussed this move with my family?
4. What abilities do I have that I can use in a prison ministry?

6
Working Your Witness

The pastor has approved your prison ministry project and has apointed you to lead. (Someone has to, and you were the one who brought the subject up!) Arrangements have been made with the institution you are to visit. Now what? The suggestions in this chapter are a sort of smorgasbord. Some will apply in one setting, but not another. Pick and choose, keeping in mind the facilities you will be in, the people on your team, the time you have, and the arrangements you have made with the chaplain (or official if there is no chaplain).

Start small. You may very well do your recruiting personally by just asking people if they would have an interest. Another approach would be an announcement in the church bulletin:

JACKSON COUNTY JAIL SERVICES

Our church is planning a regular jail ministry. If you are interested, meet with us at 6:45 Wednesday, October 17.
—Wendell Kelly, Leader

If, at your first meeting, you are overwhelmed with candidates, say 25, and you need only three or four—five at most—keep cool. Have everyone sit down together and sign a register—name, address, telephone number. Then explain what you plan to do, the time and day, and the frequency of your ministry. Inquire if any would find the time and day inconvenient. Make an appropriate note beside the names of any who respond. Then ask for any who have had prison ministry experience. Flag their names. Ask if any plays a musical instrument, has had personal witnessing experience, or is an ex-offender. (Ex-offenders make highly motivated workers. They may encounter entry problems at some institutions, however.) Has any had small-group experience? Bible teaching? Are any willing to correspond with a prisoner?

This will give you a basis for screening your candidates. Tell the group you can only use five (or however many) and you will go over the names with the pastoral staff, then call them. Those whose names are not called should be kept on file for substitutions and for additional teams. Encourage all to attend a special prayer service for prison ministry.

As soon as your program becomes stabilized, include your backup personnel in actual prison ministry from time to time.

At the beginning, your structure can be completely informal. Later, as teams multiply or follow-up activities are developed, more formal structure can be added. Mix-ups in communication and failure to get things done are clues that more attention needs to be paid to organization. The chaplain, pastor, or Christian education director can help you develop a suitable organizational plan.

Before proceeding to the content of your ministry, it might be helpful to discuss the kinds of people who make effective prison workers. I discovered early that I was no judge of who would make an effective worker. Soon after my wife and I became involved in prison work, our leader casually mentioned he was going to ask my mother-in-law to come along. She was a gracious lady of wide experience and almost 70 years old. But she had spent practically her whole life in church. Frankly, I thought she had been too sheltered to relate to men in prison—or they to her. I just couldn't see her sitting in a smoke-filled room where the language sometimes got rough in a tense discussion.

How wrong I was! Almost overnight she became "Mom" to everyone, even the warden. She was everyone's favorite confidante, the sainted mother all wished they'd had. A black brother said it all—and left the congregation in laughter—when he stood to testify: "I'm so glad to be in this place with Mom back there. You know, she looks just like my mother!"

The setting of your ministry will make a difference in the people you can use. If you must keep apart as a group and present a program from a platform, then the ability to speak or sing is important. But if you conduct small groups and have opportunity for one-on-one contact, public speaking ability is not a requisite. Any person who is at ease among inmates and able to express genuine concern can be effective. Naturally someone who is unstable in his Christian experience would be a liability, as would someone going along just for kicks.

Should women have a part in your ministry? The institution may answer the question for you. There is no doubt that using women as volunteers in ministry to a male population raises a whole new set of considerations. Even the inmates will voice differing opinions. Some (admittedly few) will say the very presence of women is too provocative. They can't handle it. For most it restores a sense of reality, a touch of the world outside where normal relationships hold.

There are men who come to religious activities when women are present who would not come otherwise. More than once a man has testified, "I came to see the women. I got saved." Before you hasten to judgment, consider that most of the men react the same way toward children. At Christmastime one institution has an inmate-staff party to which employees and community volunteers may bring their families. It is a moving experience to see a man hold a child and say, "My Debbie must be like this now."

The illustration of the children should not divert us from some legitimate concerns, however, the highest standards of conduct and dress should be insisted upon. Husband-and-wife teams can be effective. They add the extra dimension of modeling good man-woman relationships. My wife has shared my prison ministry almost from the beginning.

Romantic involvements may develop. The young woman who before-the-fact would have rejected such a possibility may find herself emotionally committed to a man with years yet to spend behind bars. We are not suggesting women are more vulnerable than men. It's just that most prison ministry is in institutions for men.

You must judge your own situation. Men in prison

are not animals. Most are highly protective of their guests from outside. Simply be prudent.

A strong camaraderie develops among people sharing prison ministry. It transcends social and economic backgrounds. Consequently, your team may drift into harmful attitudes. It is easy to become a clique. This happens with many groups, particularly in a large church. Doing things together makes us special to each other. There are ways of keeping this from becoming extreme. Deliberately build relationships with the rest of the church. The next chapter will discuss this in more detail.

Tailor the following ideas and descriptions to fit your situation. If you discover an effective format, don't hesitate to make it the backbone of your ministry. In institutions with frequent turnover, like a county jail, you can recycle your program indefinitely. But your team needs the stimulation of new ideas and fresh approaches, so introduce variety for their sake if nothing else.

The classic format used in many jails without chapel facilities is really the same as the old-fashioned street meeting. You move into a hallway or other open area and conduct a short service. Typically it will include music, prayer, testimonies, and a short message, concluding with appeal. If the situation allows, the team may split up to talk with inmates individually and pass out literature. As always, you must follow carefully the policy of the institution. If there is no open area and you have to go into different tanks, you will, in effect, need a team for each tank.

Songbooks encourage inmate participation in a

service such as this. The institution may object to your bringing in songbooks every time, but accept the idea of leaving a small supply of books on the premises to be picked up and distributed for the service. (Don't push the institutional staff to expand your ministry at the beginning. First, build respect, *then* ask for favors if need be.)

You may hear an inmate singing with obvious enthusiasm. Invite him to sing one verse as a solo while your group hums. If a man has made a commitment, let him give his testimony. Even in a situation where complete separation is maintained, try to encourage inmates to feel a part of the service. Don't say, "Now all you convicts join in!" Such language is divisive even as it invites participation. Rather use inclusive phrases like "shall we," "let's all," and "everybody join."

As with any subculture, the prison world has its own jargon. Volunteers sometimes try to achieve acceptance by adopting this vocabulary. It is doubtful whether much is gained by using it. Understand as much of it as possible, but exercise care in using it. For one thing, the jargon is not universal. Also, it is in a constant state of change, just as any slang. Then there may be subtle nuances you miss that could make you sound like a fool if you aren't aware of them. Should you find the institution where you work is sensitive to certain usages, by all means observe the preferences current there. For example, "prisoner" and "inmate" may be taboo. "Resident" may be the favored word. The institution may "incarcerate" rather than "imprison."

Exaggerated attempts to identify with the audience are always inappropriate. Unless you have been incarcerated yourself, don't say, "I know how you feel," in reference to their confinement. They won't believe you.

Nor does every illustration used have to remind inmates they are in jail or prison. The same approaches that are effective with others can touch hearts behind bars. It is easy to fall into the habit of using pat statements like, "Lots of people outside are just as much in prison as you are." (Small comfort.) I've heard it hundreds of times (more than once from my own lips). It's a true statement, but overused. If you find yourself hearing such expressions over and over, curb your own use of them.

The prayer time can be an effective way to bring people from diverse backgrounds to unity. Take requests from everyone, including the team. When one of the volunteers says, "Please pray for my sister. She has just discovered she has cancer," the man behind bars says to himself, "These people are hurting too. Yet they come out here to sing and pray and talk to me." There is no more powerful sharing.

When holding services in an institution with a chapel and a chaplain, have a clear understanding of what is permitted. Can volunteers sit in the congregation with inmates? Can team members mix with the audience at the concluding prayer time? One chaplain discouraged emotional altar calls. The institution had some inmates with psychiatric problems he feared would be aggravated by strong appeals. His successor on the other hand encouraged altar calls. In a spirit of "all things to all people" our team cooperated fully with both. An interesting sidelight was the testimony of a nonbelieving psychiatrist who said he had never seen a patient harmed by exposure to a strong religious appeal.

Should your team be conducting only a part of a

service that is under the direction of someone else, have a clear understanding of your time limit and observe it scrupulously.

Music ministry is often the "open sesame" in prison work. If your team itself has musical talent, so much the better. You can intersperse special music with other activities using your own people. If not, arrange to bring in special groups. Never, however, show up at the gate with a 16-piece band and a truckload of instruments and sound equipment without getting clearance well ahead (days or weeks) of time. Many institutions have a surplus of musical groups at Christmas and Easter, when churches have lots of special music prepared and are looking for extra opportunities to perform. It may not be the case where you minister, though. Your church choir's Christmas or Easter cantata may be welcomed. Don't forget—prisons are no different from churches. It is easy to become caught up in presenting a "program" when the real need is to share a worship experience.

Well-known gospel groups appearing at your church may be willing to present a prison concert. Chaplains are sometimes not aware such groups are in town and would welcome your assistance in arranging an appearance. It is necessary to make advance arrangements with the chaplain.

If your institution has the equipment, or you can furnish it, a religious tape and record library can be a blessing. Sermon tapes can be included. If there is no chaplain, ideas like this are not enthusiastically received. They simply represent another bother for an already overworked staff. It doesn't hurt to ask, though.

An early evening hymn sing and sharing time has been one of the most effective tools our team has used. It started with just a small group of inmates around the piano, with a couple of volunteers—one to play the piano and one to act as sponsor. It grew to include a number of volunteers and inmates, with testimonies, prayer time, and other features. Preaching is generally confined to remarks between songs and an appeal at the close. Sharing time has occasionally included some strange testimonies and unusual special music, but we are inclined to be tolerant unless someone is really disruptive.

Interspersed with a great deal of variety are some traditional features that give continuity. For example, after the final prayer time, which includes prayer for salvation, for men leaving the institution, and for physical healing, the whole congregation stands together, often holding hands, to sing the Lord's Prayer. It is usually the concluding song even on Inmate Night, when all the music and most of the testimonies are provided by the men themselves.

A number of activities are adaptable to either team or individual use. If you can't have a service, either because of your limitations or the institution situation, suggest a regular Bible study. A Bible study may involve only one volunteer and one inmate, or a dozen volunteers and inmates may participate. Adapt the content and teaching method to the circumstances. If you have the same inmates week after week, a continued study is good (such as the Prison Bible Course available through the Assemblies of God). If there is a high turnover in population, studies complete in one session might be preferable.

A series on familiar passages gives a sense of relationship even though each study stands on its own. For example, John 3:16 makes an excellent salvation study. Follow this with a study on the Lord's Prayer.

Talk about the new believer learning to pray, his new family relationship to the Father, etc. The 23rd Psalm with its message of assurance could follow.

Regular Sunday school materials are excellent. Many undated studies are available in both student and teacher manuals. Discussion is good. Having a team member or two in the class with you helps both stimulate and control discussion. The class setting can include sharing of experiences, prayer, and encouragement to accept Christ.

You will have men with varied backgrounds and differing interpretations of Scripture. Treat them with respect. In any group you are likely to have one or two who will dominate. Establishing ground rules will help: for example, everyone gets a chance to talk before anyone talks twice.

The text for this book (Matthew 25) suggests another role you and your team may play: "... *and you visited me.*" Just coming to talk as a friend can be an important ministry. You are not preaching. You are not trying to reform. You simply accept the inmate as he is. You may only listen without offering advice. Soon enough he will ask you questions. He will want to know where you are "coming from." Slowly you can share appropriate experiences, both spiritual and secular. Slowly—don't overwhelm him with intimacy. As you talk about your family, your work, and your church, he vicariously shares your life. You may feel an urgency that makes this slow, casual approach seem like a luxury you can't afford. If he is transient, you may wish to witness more directly.

Unless you have had training, don't assume a counseling role. For you, the activities described above will be sufficient. One technique you can use is really a listening technique. Rather than directly commenting on what is said, you simply replay what has been said, with emphasis on the feelings involved. For example, the inmate says: "My dad was always putting me down. I could never do anything to please him. Finally I just said, 'If that's the way you feel, I'll show you....'" You might reply: "I hear you saying you really wanted your father's approval and it hurt you deeply when he didn't respond...."

Often, as you talk, the inmate will work out solutions to his own problems.

This brings up the whole question of sensitivity. When do I talk? When do I listen? When do I witness? The biggest hurdle most of us have to get over in these matters is our own perception of what constitutes witnessing. If witnessing means only laying down the "four spiritual laws" or quoting John 3:16, then we will come away from a low-key friendly-visit approach kicking ourselves and feeling guilty. And indeed, if it was only fear that prevented our making a more direct witness, maybe we should be dismayed.

On the other hand, if we see the very fact that we are there inside the prison as a witness—as Christ's loving concern being expressed through us—we may go away satisfied even if the subject of religion is never brought up. But we have to be sure in our own hearts that our delay is truly spiritual sensitivity and part of a total strategy, rather than an excuse not to confront a sinner with his need.

Small groups are effective opportunities for ministry in prisons. Your Bible study may be considered such a group. There are many other kinds, though. In institutions with a stable population you can build such groups around special interests. Poetry is an example. You would be surprised at the number of would-be poets prison spawns!

We have had a general discussion group for years in one institution. While we aren't strict about subject, usually the discussion has some theme related to the Christian life. A current newsstory may be used to start a discussion. It can be a simple item. A clipping about children's Christmas wants can kick off a whole evening: "What one thing do *you* want more than anything else?" You can let the discussion be freewheeling, moving into other areas, or you can keep calling it back to the stated theme. Some find such a session frustrating if no conclusions are reached. Others simply enjoy the exchange of ideas.

You may be jarred by one inmate verbally attacking another in such sessions. Intervene by asking that the group keep to issues, rather than deal in personalities. Maintain control of the session and your firmness will generally be respected. Such groups work best if the moderator simply starts and guides, rather than lectures. Occasionally he may clarify tactfully, or provide continuity by harmonizing various views.

A number of books have been written on the dynamics of small groups. Many are available at Christian bookstores. In some of these, and in some secular usages, the term *small group* has a specialized, limited meaning. If this is the case, the publication will usually alert you by defining its particular usage.

A well-organized program of fellowship, study, and shared commitment called *Yokefellows* operates in many prisons. The chaplain might suggest that you and members of your group enter this program as an avenue of ministry. Its standards are high, both for inmate and volunteer, and, as its name implies, it has a strong emphasis on building relationships between Christians inside and out.

There are several activities your prison ministry might sponsor that would involve the entire church. One is a correspondence ministry. (Please, not *pen* pals!) There are men in prison who have no one. They never get a letter. If your team knows of such people, you can arrange for members of your church to write. First, however, clear such a project with the chaplain or the representative of the institution with whom you deal.

There are men in prison who glean names from every available source and carry on correspondence with literally hundreds of people. Their purposes may be entirely innocent. On the other hand, they may gently milk all their correspondents—a dollar here, five there. Some carry on multiple romances. It is a game with them, but heartbreak for lonely girls. Sadly, the exploitation works both ways. With the boy behind bars, a girl figures a little paper romance won't hurt anybody, and leads the man to believe he may have a future with her to look forward to outside. Again, proceed with caution. Some institutions frown on volunteers initiating such programs.

The same men who receive no letters will likely receive no visits. Churches—even whole communities—carry on "family adoption" programs. A family in the church "adopts" an inmate. They visit him in the visiting room of the institution, write, and generally treat him as a friend. Such a program thoughtfully administered, can be a blessing both to the families and the men. Again, clear it with the institution first.

"Family adoption" may also describe an entirely different kind of program your whole church may embark on. Families of men in prison suffer deeply. The hurt is both emotional and economic. It is a time when they need desperately to be loved and respected. Temptations abound. Your church can take such a family under its wing and expand your ministry. The mother, the children, and the father in prison can all be ministered to in this way.

Now may be the time to insert some words of warning before going on to other aspects of your witness. You never give love without opening yourself to the possibility of being hurt. When you love the unloved, the risk is doubled. It should come as no surprise that you will encounter people in your prison ministry who will seek to use and manipulate you. Your church may have some disillusioning experiences as it attempts to back you in your ministry by reaching out with you to families and to men coming out of prison. Consciously letting someone take advantage of you may not be an expression of love. It may be more loving to say, "This is wrong. I'm not going to let you do this to me." But abandoning someone because you've been hurt or, worse still, dropping a desperately needed ministry because of a few bad experiences, is hardly the path of love either.

So far we have discussed your prison ministry mostly in terms of the inmates and your relationships with them. Almost as important is the way you relate to the jailer, the guard, the staff member, and the chaplain.

For a long time after our team started its prison ministry, we unconsciously treated the prison staff like nonpersons. Without realizing it we had so identified with the "us versus them" psychology of the inmates that we hardly even spoke to the staff. One day the chaplain called it to our attention. "You know, those men think you religious volunteers snub them. You laugh and shake hands and talk with the inmates, yet you never even speak to the officers."

Since then we have made an effort to cultivate our relationships with the staff. We have discovered some who are Christians. These men face terrific peer pressure. A man who is identified as weak or too friendly to inmates is seen as a threat to the security of the men he works with. The old nonsense that Christians are weak still persists. Even if the officers are friendly, don't be surprised if your reception is cool. You are an outsider in their world in more ways than one.

Relating to the chaplain is an entirely different matter. You see him as the pastor in charge of the area where you are working. In this role the chaplain is very concerned that the spiritual needs of the inmates are met. He realizes he may be limited in reaching their many different needs. This is where the volunteer can effectively serve to help complete the religious program. The volunteer, in this relationship, becomes an extension of the chaplain.

The chaplain sees you in one of two roles. You come to the institution to serve as a member of the chaplain's team in ministry, or you come to do your own thing on his turf. There is room in prison work for the latter, but try to understand where you fit in the total picture. It sometimes comes as a shock to volunteers from a local church who have been conducting a Friday evening Bible class for a year to discover there are 47 other religious volunteers of every faith with activities going on every day of the week. Knowing that another denomination with contradicting views conducts services twice a week may explain why you get some of the questions you do. An inquiry to the chaplain or a request for a schedule of religious activities will give you the overall picture you need.

Probably you will discover a core of activities the chaplain considers *his* program. These are meetings of various kinds that he has initiated, recruited volunteers for, and directly oversees. More than likely the Sunday morning worship will be his service. By knowing what his program is you can avoid usurping or undermining it. You may encounter a chaplain who fits none of your criteria for spirituality. You may even doubt he is a Christian. Or he may have theological views opposing yours that he voices strongly. Accept his authority graciously and carry on your ministry as cooperatively as possible. Pray for him.

The real temptation will come when inmates start complaining about the chaplain's faults. You must be aware that he is often the focus of discontent simply because he represents a kind of relief valve in a pressure situation. Avoid reinforcing their gripes by agreeing. If the complaints deal with character and effectiveness, suggest they discuss their problems with him, then commit the matter to prayer. If the complaint has to do with doctrinal matters, simply suggest he is representing his personal view and drop it.

Sometimes the gripe will be directed at the program. "We want to have an inmates' charismatic prayer group and he turned thumbs down." You may feel an inmates' charismatic prayer meeting is just what the institution needs and be tempted to say it is too bad the chaplain isn't sensitive to the Spirit. Such a remark would be a put-down to the chaplain and would build you up a bit by demonstrating you were allied with the inmates and *you* were sensitive to the Spirit. But it would be divisive.

A little investigation might reveal the chaplain had good reason to hesitate. He may have had genuine scheduling problems. Or he may have been battling some attitudes of spiritual snobbery that were threatening the unity of the Christian community and he questioned the timeliness of the move.

Counsel the inmates who come to you for guidance about the various shades of doctrine and practices they encounter to be true to the Word and their convictions, yet loving and supportive of other Christian brothers. In a setting where you encounter many shades of opinion, this advice goes for volunteers too.

If you are carrying out the ministry in the institution as an integral part of the chaplain's program, your relationship with him may be quite different. He becomes your pastor while you are working there. You owe him and his objectives loyalty. Your style will be in keeping with the Christian message he wants to project. Obviously you will have some frank discussions with him before you assume this relationship.

For many years a number of us have worked in this way with chaplains of other denominations. We have shared deep fellowship with them. Undoubtedly this was possible because our real goal—to win men to Christ and to help them grow—was the same. Should that change, we would have to reassess our position. The posture we have taken has contributed to a strong sense of unity within the "inside Christian community." We minister in the many ways mentioned elsewhere in this chapter. We participate in morning chapel, conduct hymn sings and sharing times, have small groups and Bible studies, and do one-on-one counseling. Except for the Sunday morning chapel, many of the activities are led by volunteers. Inmates know our local church affiliation, just as they know the chaplain's denomination, but they consider us all a part of their church.

In this institution, at this time, with the people now involved, it works and works well.

In some large institutions with a stable population there is, in effect, an actual inmate church, clearly organized, with standards for membership and set qualifications for various offices. If such a church is active in your institution, the chaplain will help you in relating your ministry to it. One such inmate church has members who have prepared themselves for the ministry after their conversion behind bars.

From time to time throughout the book we have put out caution flags. Even though it has been touched on elsewhere, it may be well to conclude this chapter with a warning about your attitudes.

It is simplistic to say (as we did in chapter 3) that these are "just people like everybody else." Many are. But there are people in prison—charming people—whose whole life has been spent using other people, living utterly selfishly, with no regard for anyone else. It is too weak to say, "You *may* be fooled." You *will* be fooled if you spend much time in prison ministry. You will be confronted with liars—people who compulsively distort the truth.

People who know more about the Bible than you do will try to "club" you with it. Your friendship and confidence will be wooed, and then you will be viciously attacked—not physically, but psychologically and verbally—by the very one you tried to help.

Even those you have come to regard as "good guys" may crush you by expecting more than you can possibly deliver, then accusing you of letting them down and being less than a Christian.

You may, consequently, find yourself going through a sequence of changing attitudes. Initially you wholly identify with these brothers in bondage. It is your idealistic period. Then you get hurt—emotionally, maybe even financially. Disappointment sets in. Realism is your attitude at this stage. Ultimately you may encounter enough disappointments that cynicism begins to mar your attitude. That will be a time to reassess.

There is nothing wrong with identifying. Just don't let it blind you. Be realistic. Keep your ministry Christ-centered, remembering the people you work with are in His hands. That takes the edge off disappointments. The involvement of your own ego is what makes getting hurt so painful. We can be so personally proud of *our* protege's progress that we feel unduly let down at his failures. The Christ-centered approach will help you avoid cynicism too. You can't focus on Him without gaining a fresh infusion of His compassion.

Questions to Ask Yourself

1. Could I handle a leadership role in a prison ministry?
2. Would I be faithful in some nonleadership role?
3. What strengths do I have that would help me in this kind of activity?
4. What are the names of five people who might join me in this endeavor?
5. I am imagining myself introducing myself and testifying to a group of inmates for the first time. Here is what I would say:

7

Accountability

Phil was a real trophy of God's grace. He was the classic convict—a guy who had done it all and looked it. He was tough and used colorful language, but with a certain appealing style, and was true to the convicts' code. He found Jesus and got a parole too. Everyone involved in prison ministry was proud of Phil, including the chaplain.

Things appeared to go well outside. He was invited to speak at men's meetings in churches. He wrote letters to the editor about prison conditions. He had job opportunities, but he never settled down in one church. Little question marks began to develop. A brother in one congregation had made a small loan. Phil hadn't been back since. He had contracted to do some painting, with part of the pay in advance. It wasn't getting done. A woman was apparently a live-in guest at his apartment—without benefit of a marriage license. Finally word got back to the inmates in the institution. "All that support, and Phil blew it. He's ruined it for the rest of us!"

It's easy to outline Phil's responsibilities. In his

new life he became the representative of a lot of people. He had a responsibility to God, to the chaplain, to the other Christian workers, to the churches of the community that received him, and especially to his inmate brothers whose own chances hung on his success. Poor old Phil just wasn't equal to such a load. Not in himself. He's back inside again.

In this chapter we're not going to talk further about Phil's responsibilities, though. He just happened to be a good example of how interlinked we all are as Christians. It's your accountability as a volunteer in prison ministry we want to discuss.

Accountability and responsibility are not negative, burdensome words. They really are descriptive words spotlighting one aspect of a transaction. We become accountable because we have received something. Accountability is one side of the bargain. Let's start with your church.

When you become a volunteer, the church you represent makes a considerable investment in your ministry, even if it never spends a dime. The church clothes you with its hard-earned reputation in the community. You are trading on its good name. The church invests in your ministry in other ways. As a missionary sent by it you can expect prayer support, understanding, and sharing of concern.

It is not enough, though, that you simply go about your ministry without bringing shame on the church. As the word *accountability* itself suggests, there is a reporting back that is essential to making your church feel its trust in you has paid off. Without being pushy, seek opportunities for sharing what God is doing. There will be opportunities in prayer meetings, testimony and sharing times, Sunday school, and small-group meetings. Share your prayer burdens with the congregation as well as your victories.

Part of your total responsibility to all of prison ministry, to inmates, and particularly to the church itself, is to be an educator. Christian people outside especially need to have their prison consciousness heightened. Ninety-seven percent of the people in prisons and jails return to the community. Of these, some will have made a Christian start during this low point in their lives. Most churches are not anxious to receive and nurture converts of this kind. You owe it to your church (as your church owes it to the Christian ex-offender) to help it open itself to this kind of ministry.

Prison volunteers may be just little fingers in the body of believers, but the church deserves a continuous awareness that those fingers are alive and functioning. This does not mean you should monopolize every conversation with accounts of prison ministry (although it's tempting!). We are all likely to see the area of *our* concern as the world's most needy mission field.

Even if by some means you become involved in prison ministry on your own, and not as an appointed representative of your church, you haven't escaped responsibility. As long as you are known to be a member of a church or denomination, you have an obligation to conduct yourself in your ministry with consideration for your church. Share your burden. Keep your pastor and church informed. You will build interest and perhaps pave the way for formal church involvement.

Another very clearly defined responsibility is to the chaplain or other institutional representative who gives you access. He literally puts his job and his reputation in his special community on the line when he lets you in.

You are not obligated to agree with him. But you must respectfully follow his instructions. As we have mentioned in earlier chapters, it is a grave breach of trust to use your access to undermine the chaplain's reputation or to discredit his programs. Inmate confidence is difficult enough for him to build without your words or attitudes undermining him.

It is in the area of responsibility to the institution that you may find inner conflict. As you work with inmates, you develop a loyalty to them. You sympathize with their objectives. This is natural. In gaining access to the institution, you agree to abide by its regulations. Often they are actually laws of the land. The inmate has made no such agreement. Even Christian inmates sometimes rationalize away any obligation to play by the adversary's rules.

What are your duties when you become aware of infractions? The revelation may come in the course of a sensitive and confidential counseling relationship. Yet you are not a priest or a psychiatrist whose profession gives him privilege. Do you violate the confidence of the inmate or the institution? It is one of those dilemmas of conscience life throws at us.

You may have been forewarned if the institution gave you an orientation lecture. You will likely have been told a condition of your entry is that you would report promptly any illegal or questionable approach made to you. If you sense an inmate is about to involve you in such a matter in some way, you can forestall it by simply saying, "Look, Bill, I am obligated by my agreement in coming in here to reveal any illegal approaches made to me. Please don't tell me something I don't want to hear."

It is not beyond possibility that in the course of dealing with a man about his soul he will say, "You have to help me. I have killed a man and I'm afraid I'll do it again." However much you would like to be the instrument of change, you are in over your depth in such a situation. Give the man every assurance of your love and concern and of God's desire to forgive and His power to keep. But share the incident immediately with the chaplain. Not only do you have legal obligation to do so—the safety of other people, the security of the institution, and the future of volunteer ministry may hinge on the way you handle yourself. An approach you could make to the chaplain might be, "Chaplain, in dealing with one of the men, he revealed a fear he might kill someone. He told me this in confidence, and while I don't want to betray that confidence, I felt in over my depth." The chaplain may very well take it from there. He may already be aware of the situation. He certainly can guide you in handling yourself correctly, helping you resolve the issue of confidence versus the safety of all, including that of the man himself.

This illustration is of course extreme. Suffice it to say you should resist playing either the role of psychiatrist or policeman.

There are other ways your responsibility to the future of all volunteer ministry must be discharged. Naturally all of your relationships with the institution and its personnel are important. The temptation on the institution's part is always strong to eliminate any program that seems more bothersome than it is worth. Consistency is essential—just being on time; keeping a regular schedule; and being plain, old-fashioned dependable. Squabbles within your own group or tensions in relation to the sponsoring church that are apparent to the chaplain or institution serve to discredit your ministry and make it that much harder for volunteers in the future.

Inmates too deserve more from your team than spillover of conflict among its members or differences with the chaplain. Many people in prison already have a negative picture of the church. Hypocrisy, bickering, and holier-than-thou attitudes characterize their perception of the religious world. All of your behavior in the institution must be consistent with your professed reasons for being there.

This ministry, as all ministries, owes its final accountability to the Lord. Tacked up on the wall of your inner meditation chamber should be this paraphrase of 1 Corinthians 13:1-3: "Though I do all these things and put in all these hours of prison ministry at personal sacrifice—without love, it is nothing."

Often as we reach the locked grill that closes off the chapel area in our institution, a knot of men will be waiting, anxious to greet our volunteers and shake hands before the service begins. I have no idea what Jesus looks like—how tall or short, or how old. But sometimes in my mind's eye I see Him waiting for us just inside the bars with these men.

"Hey," Jesus says, "you came!"

I'm not surprised to find Him there. That's how He said it would be.

Questions to Ask Yourself

1. Is there such a thing as an "independent" ministry?
2. What if I feel institutional guidelines are wrong or harmful?
3. What is my responsibility to my own family when

I become involved in an activity like prison ministry?
4. Is it all right to take part in something like this just for the experience, even though I don't have a deep interest in it?
5. How much should I talk about the strange, funny, and shocking things I see and hear?

8
Follow Up

Donald was one of those people who always seemed like a kid. A bit too eager to please, a bit too dependent, and subject to emotional swings. Sometimes he seemed quite intelligent; other times you wondered. Donald was always at the services, always helpful, and always needing reassurance. "I was just looking at a city map. Think I know about where you live. You know, I'm going to be getting out next month. We'll have some good times together out there, won't we? You will be my friend, won'tcha? 'Cause I don't have anybody at all We can go to your church and you can introduce me to a nice girl. I told you, didn't I, that my wife got a divorce? She took the kids and everything. I'm not even going to get to see 'em. You won't forget me now, will ya?"

The words of reassurance, friendship, and love come so easily when you know in a few minutes the iron gates will close behind you and you'll go home; all your "good buddies" locked safely away. But one Saturday morning when you had planned to sleep late, fix the garage door, and watch the championship game on TV, the telephone rings. "Hi! I finished my parole. I'm back in town—right here at the bus station."

"Bill who? Oh, yes, that Bill."

He's the Bill you prayed with and encouraged when he made a commitment. Now he's back—a free man. You're his Christian friend. No, he doesn't have any money; no place to stay, no job. And there's one thing you should know—he does have this girl with him!

At the very beginning of our involvement in prison ministry a minor crisis developed in this very area. Maybe even a major crisis. I had to decide whether I was a hypocrite or not. Would I talk about the love of Christ and assume the role of a representative of that love while I was inside the prison, if I were not prepared to be exactly the same person outside? Now, before you ever become involved with prison ministry, is the time to answer that question.

Many of us have problems in the area of personal witnessing. Could it be that subconsciously we don't want to assume the burden of nurturing the new babes our witnessing brings into the world? If we could just tell them about salvation and go our way.... But all of us, if we have any sensitivity, know our witness shouldn't end there. We need to be friends to all new believers, include them in our circle, and spend time with them as they face problems. We must be brother and sister, father and mother to them. And they may not even be "our type." Really, deep down we may not even like them.

We would rather build our church community with timber of our own choosing—people we like, whose economic, ethnic, or educational status does not embarrass us. It is in succumbing to these very real feelings that we quit witnessing, withdraw from serving the world in need, and model our Christian fellowships into comfortable retreats. We still have our tokens—the baskets we distribute on holidays and our missions offerings. But deep down a deadness has set in because we'd rather sit at the table than wash humanity's feet.

Your prison involvement will bring all this down on you in a hurry. Be prepared. The problems are real. You cannot do the job alone. That is why it is important to cultivate the full support of your pastor and the entire congregation. They must begin to share your attitude of reaching out and concern.

You and your church can get involved immediately and get a full cross section of what it's all about by ministering to the families of men in prison. As with all your activities, clear this with the chaplain or institution.

Betty was Dick's second wife. She had two children and Dick had two when they were married. Dick had drinking problems and was out of work when arrested. He was abusive when drunk and their marriage was troubled. Now he is in prison. They are trying to hold the marriage together although neither one is sure just why. Betty is on welfare. She has been evicted from two apartments because of the children. Boyfriends come by occasionally and she leaves the children alone while she goes out. Years ago she was a Christian and she weeps as she talks about her Christian mother and those earlier times. Right now she is most interested in getting a place to live.

In just one situation like this you and your church will face some fundamental questions of what being a Christian is all about. How you answer may have a great deal to say about whether you have any business being involved in prison ministry.

Let's say, though, that you are willing to open yourself a little to unpleasantness, hurt, and disillusionment. What about the man coming out of prison then?

There are several ways a man can get out besides escaping. Most obvious, he can finish his sentence. Even "doing it all" seldom means staying the full length of the sentence. Most institutions have "good time" provisions. For each month completed without incident or infraction of rules a certain amount of time is deducted from the sentence. This time is awarded by statute, But at the discretion of the institution, it may be deducted as an enforcement tool. A man who violates the rules can lose "good time." There are also provisions for reinstatement of time lost.

Most inmates go out on parole. After completing a prescribed part of their sentence, they are eligible to go before the parole board. If granted parole, the offender is released conditionally. Among the conditions, he must report regularly to a parole officer until his sentence is completed. He must not associate with ex-felons. He cannot leave a prescribed area without permission, etc. The halfway house, when available, is sometimes used as an intermediate step.

Some restrictions may follow an ex-offender even after his sentence is completed and he is discharged from parole. The restrictions vary, but usually include loss of voting rights and the right to own weapons, loss of license to practice certain professions, etc. Convictions of misdemeanors do not carry these penalties of course.

A bit of roleplaying may better give you the feel of what this chapter is all about. Recall the most embarrassing, shameful episode in your life—one of those times when you wished the earth would swallow you, when you just knew no one would ever speak to you again. Imagine that immediately after this incident you went away for a year. You lost your job, left all your family behind, and spent the entire year constantly reminded of that shameful episode. Now suddenly you are back in your hometown, getting off the bus. You have only the clothes on your back and $50. You have nowhere to stay, no job, and no prospects. The feelings you have generated in this roleplay are simply a shadow of the real-life despair men and women leaving prison face every day.

There are certain needs almost all ex-offenders share: housing, a job, vocational training, family counseling, help with addiction problems, financial counseling, friends, and acceptance. The Christian ex-offender needs all this and more. He needs to be received in a local church that is nurturing and supportive so he can develop spiritually. The church must understand that freedom in itself constitutes a problem for many ex-offenders. Handling it responsibily requires learning new techniques. It is a process demanding patience on everyone's part.

For secular needs there are a number of government and community agencies waiting to help. We will mention them as we go further. Unfortunately, the ex-offender may never arrive at their doors. For many a man the only thing on his mind, to use his own phrase, is a "beer and a broad." With alcohol addiction playing such a major role in many inmates' lives, it is not surprising that a common experience of releasees is to sober up from their first drinking bout and find themselves on their way back to prison.

"But," you protest, "I would only be involved with men who have made a Christian commitment." The bottle may well be *their* first battle too.

Ralph was an intelligent young man who had worked through deep emotional problems while in prison. Much of his progress grew out of yielding his life to the Lord. He was apprehensive about his release—the "shortitus" that men whose time is coming to an end usually suffer—and somewhat unrealistic in his expectations. He had begun to think of himself as a writer, and it was his hope he might find a religious publisher who would use his services. Christian friends located him a maintenance job with a religious organization that had very specific policies about smoking and drinking. He lived alone in a vacant building in return for acting as night watchman.

As time went by it became apparent he was not too happy. He had not really found a local church where he was comfortable, and he expressed discontentment with his job. The strictures against smoking and drinking, he felt, were not in keeping with the Biblical requirements of Christian living.

A late night call to one of the Christian friends brought the whole matter to a head. Ralph was talking of suicide. The weight gain that friends had laughingly attributed to "being outside agrees with you" had really resulted from the heavy beer drinking he had been doing every night. After a long talk he agreed to sign himself into a local hospital as an alcoholic patient.

Ralph lost his job and his place to stay. He could

not bring himself to seek a dishwashing job or some other temporary employment. Since the terms of his parole called for him to be gainfully employed, he was sent back to the state from which he had come.

The last word was Ralph was still battling his drinking, still occasionally attending church, and still counting himself a Christian, although not an overcoming Christian.

Lots of questions are raised by people like Ralph. How patient is God? How many stumbles and false starts will He forgive? What is clear is that few churches are prepared to handle such ups and downs.

Two or three volunteers undertaking to work with an individual can soon find themselves pressed to the limit. With already heavy schedules, it is hard to crowd in a whole evening helping someone pray through again, acting as an intermediary in a family split-up. Even if you are trying to involve professional counselors, you may wind up persuading, pleading, and praying to get the ex-offender there.

What should your role be? How can you help? Start well before release. Be sure you know as many facts as possible. The chaplain and institutional social workers should know of your desire to help before you even discuss it with the inmate. Involve as many others as you can. Learn about the man's background and his family situation. An unsaved wife who wants no part of her husband's new commitment can present a serious problem. What are his job skills? his education? Then you can begin to check community services to meet his secular needs: vocational training programs for ex-offenders, job placement services, etc.

Talk with your pastor to find out what kind of

reception the man can expect in the church. His marital status may be important to the church. If he is young and single, people may become protective of the girls in the church. If he is divorced, they may envision even more problems. There is no point in keeping fears and reservations about such things secret. Talk them out. Face facts honestly.

Your personal role should be that of Christian friend and introducer. Don't become a crutch. You should be available, but do not smother the ex-offender. He may become paranoid if you hover over his shoulder constantly. Encourage self-reliance. Don't get started down the road of financial involvement. It is better that financial assistance, if given at all, be a group action or channeled through the church. Be aware that your own guilt feelings—"I haven't done enough"—can set you up to be exploited. This is why it is important to act as a group. It makes it easier to be objective in problem situations.

There may be matters that require professional help. Make use of Christian counseling services when needed. Overconfidence and unreasonable expectations can swamp both volunteer and the ex-offender. Encourage a careful, day-by-day, step-by-step approach.

Is it worth it all? Just from a purely financial standpoint, every person kept out of prison saves from $5,000 to $15,000 a year in the direct costs of incarceration. This doesn't include the welfare expense and the human costs to the family, or the loss of taxes and other economic contributions the person would have made if gainfully employed. Only God can place a value on the spiritual fruits of such an endeavor.

Discouragement may dog you in between victories in this kind of effort. You will be hurt. Aren't most parents and friends? It is the price of love. Just remember, an 80-percent success rate (and that is phenomenal) means 2 out of every 10 fail. Even God, starting with an untarnished pair who had a perfect heritage and a perfect environment, lost them both. And He still hasn't given up.

We mustn't either.

Questions to Ask Yourself

1. Even if I just did prison ministry and didn't get involved in follow-up, wouldn't that be worthwhile?
2. Are these people really saved who have problems like this chapter talks about?
3. Can I count on my Christian circle to share with me in ministering to ex-offenders? Will they be accepting and open?
4. Do I know anything about the various social services in my community?

9
The Rewards

By now you may be quoting chapter 1 and saying, "He's right. Prison ministry is not for everyone. And it's not for me."

In my desire not to glamorize or oversell, I have not given much emphasis to the rewards. And even now, this is going to be the shortest chapter in the book! The truth is that over and over again volunteers go into prison ministry thinking, "I'll go into this dark place and take in some light and hope and cheer." Then they come out to testify, "I got more than I gave."

Ruth (Mom) Carter, the mother-in-law I didn't think would make it as a prison volunteer, had been a pastor's wife, a minister in her own right, a foreign and home missionary, and a Bible college matron. "Without doubt," she says, "the prison is the most rewarding ministry I have ever had."

Another volunteer said, "This opportunity for prison ministry came at the most difficult time of my personal life. I have never worshiped with a group who seemed to care so sincerely about my burdens and who lifted me up in prayer so faithfully."

One of the traditions in our hymn sing is to invite men who are leaving to say a farewell word. (One brother who had a lot of time said it wasn't his favorite tradition because *he* didn't get to say good-bye. But his time did come.) The common testimony is, "I am glad to be going but sorry to be leaving this fellowship. I found Christ here and got my life turned around."

How many are being reached? Maybe 10 percent in our institution. A recent survey of state and federal prisons showed a direct correlation between the number of outside volunteers and the number of inmates participating in religious activities.

There are a number of programs recruiting prison witnesses. Some are within denominational frameworks, others are interdenominational, and some are sponsored by chaplains. A local church group has some distinct advantages. For one thing, it is a chance to polish again the tarnished reputation "church" has for many inmates. Then it creates a readiness on the part of the church itself to receive into its fellowship the fruits of its own ministry. After all, almost all the inmates are going out, and it will be the local church where they will find their real place to serve and worship. It would be worth a trip to visit an active volunteer witness in some other church or community, particularly if you are thinking of starting a program from scratch. You'll find volunteers in prison ministry anxious to share. New recruits who have a sincere interest in this unusual ministry are welcomed, for the field is large, the challenge great.

Jesus put it so simply. His calls are like that. No list

of qualifications or credentials. The act of caring is self-validating. No special techniques or deep insights. He just said, "I was in prison and you visited me."

He's sitting now, in your nearest jail, waiting.